CONTENTS

 # RESEARCH

PLACES TO GO

_____
_____
_____
_____
_____
_____
_____
_____
_____
_____

PLACES TO EAT

_____
_____
_____
_____
_____
_____
_____
_____
_____
_____

 RESEARCH

THINGS TO DO

NOTES

TRAVEL CALENDAR

MONTH: ....

SUN	MON	TUE	WED	THU	FRI	SAT

Notes:

_____

_____

_____

_____

TRAVEL CALENDAR

MONTH: ....

SUN	MON	TUE	WED	THU	FRI	SAT

Notes:

_____

_____

_____

_____

 RESERVATIONS

DESTINATION: ....

Flight:	Confirmation #:
Airport:	Departing:
Airline:	Arriving:

Flight:	Confirmation #:
Airport:	Departing:
Airline:	Arriving:

Rental Car:	Confirmation #:
Rental Company:	
Pick Up:	Drop Off:

Lodging:	Confirmation #:
Check In:	Address:
Check Out:	

Notes:

_____

_____

_____

_____

 # RESERVATIONS

DESTINATION: ....

Flight:	Confirmation #:
Airport:	Departing:
Airline:	Arriving:

Flight:	Confirmation #:
Airport:	Departing:
Airline:	Arriving:

Rental Car:	Confirmation #:
Rental Company:	
Pick Up:	Drop Off:

Lodging:	Confirmation #:
Check In:	Address:
Check Out:	

Notes:

_____

_____

_____

_____

⬙ TRAVEL BUDGET

EXPENSE	BUDGET	ACTUAL

TRAVEL BUDGET

EXPENSE	BUDGET	ACTUAL

# PACKING LIST

ITEM	☑

⚑ PACKING LIST

ITEM	☑

ITINERARY

DATE: ....

SCHEDULE	
5:00 AM	
6:00 AM	
7:00 AM	
8:00 AM	
9:00 AM	
10:00 AM	
11:00 AM	
12:00 PM	
1:00 PM	
2:00 PM	
3:00 PM	
4:00 PM	
5:00 PM	
6:00 PM	
7:00 PM	
8:00 PM	
9:00 PM	
10:00 PM	
11:00 PM	
12:00 PM	

MEALS

BREAKFAST:

LUNCH:

DINNER:

ACTIVITIES

NOTES

MEMORIES

DATE: ....

ITINERARY

DATE: ....

SCHEDULE	
5:00AM	
6:00AM	
7:00AM	
8:00AM	
9:00AM	
10:00AM	
11:00AM	
12:00PM	
1:00PM	
2:00PM	
3:00PM	
4:00PM	
5:00PM	
6:00PM	
7:00PM	
8:00PM	
9:00PM	
10:00PM	
11:00PM	
12:00PM	

MEALS

BREAKFAST:

LUNCH:

DINNER:

ACTIVITIES

NOTES

MEMORIES

DATE: ....

ITINERARY

DATE: ....

SCHEDULE	
5:00 AM	
6:00 AM	
7:00 AM	
8:00 AM	
9:00 AM	
10:00 AM	
11:00 AM	
12:00 PM	
1:00 PM	
2:00 PM	
3:00 PM	
4:00 PM	
5:00 PM	
6:00 PM	
7:00 PM	
8:00 PM	
9:00 PM	
10:00 PM	
11:00 PM	
12:00 PM	

MEALS

BREAKFAST:

LUNCH:

DINNER:

ACTIVITIES

NOTES

MEMORIES

DATE: ....

 ITINERARY   DATE: ....

SCHEDULE	
5:00AM	
6:00AM	
7:00AM	
8:00AM	
9:00AM	
10:00AM	
11:00AM	
12:00PM	
1:00PM	
2:00PM	
3:00PM	
4:00PM	
5:00PM	
6:00PM	
7:00PM	
8:00PM	
9:00PM	
10:00PM	
11:00PM	
12:00PM	

MEALS

BREAKFAST:

LUNCH:

DINNER:

ACTIVITIES

NOTES

MEMORIES

ITINERARY

DATE: ....

SCHEDULE	
5:00 AM	
6:00 AM	
7:00 AM	
8:00 AM	
9:00 AM	
10:00 AM	
11:00 AM	
12:00 PM	
1:00 PM	
2:00 PM	
3:00 PM	
4:00 PM	
5:00 PM	
6:00 PM	
7:00 PM	
8:00 PM	
9:00 PM	
10:00 PM	
11:00 PM	
12:00 PM	

MEALS

BREAKFAST:

LUNCH:

DINNER:

ACTIVITIES

NOTES

MEMORIES

DATE: ....

ITINERARY

DATE: ....

SCHEDULE	
5:00 AM	
6:00 AM	
7:00 AM	
8:00 AM	
9:00 AM	
10:00 AM	
11:00 AM	
12:00 PM	
1:00 PM	
2:00 PM	
3:00 PM	
4:00 PM	
5:00 PM	
6:00 PM	
7:00 PM	
8:00 PM	
9:00 PM	
10:00 PM	
11:00 PM	
12:00 PM	

MEALS

BREAKFAST:

LUNCH:

DINNER:

ACTIVITIES

NOTES

MEMORIES

DATE:

ITINERARY

DATE: ....

SCHEDULE	
5:00 AM	
6:00 AM	
7:00 AM	
8:00 AM	
9:00 AM	
10:00 AM	
11:00 AM	
12:00 PM	
1:00 PM	
2:00 PM	
3:00 PM	
4:00 PM	
5:00 PM	
6:00 PM	
7:00 PM	
8:00 PM	
9:00 PM	
10:00 PM	
11:00 PM	
12:00 PM	

MEALS

BREAKFAST:

LUNCH:

DINNER:

ACTIVITIES

NOTES

MEMORIES

DATE: ....

ITINERARY

DATE: ....

SCHEDULE	
5:00 AM	
6:00 AM	
7:00 AM	
8:00 AM	
9:00 AM	
10:00 AM	
11:00 AM	
12:00 PM	
1:00 PM	
2:00 PM	
3:00 PM	
4:00 PM	
5:00 PM	
6:00 PM	
7:00 PM	
8:00 PM	
9:00 PM	
10:00 PM	
11:00 PM	
12:00 PM	

MEALS

BREAKFAST:

LUNCH:

DINNER:

ACTIVITIES

NOTES

MEMORIES

DATE: ....

ITINERARY

DATE: ....

SCHEDULE	
5:00 AM	
6:00 AM	
7:00 AM	
8:00 AM	
9:00 AM	
10:00 AM	
11:00 AM	
12:00 PM	
1:00 PM	
2:00 PM	
3:00 PM	
4:00 PM	
5:00 PM	
6:00 PM	
7:00 PM	
8:00 PM	
9:00 PM	
10:00 PM	
11:00 PM	
12:00 PM	

MEALS

BREAKFAST:

LUNCH:

DINNER:

ACTIVITIES

NOTES

MEMORIES

DATE: ....

 ITINERARY   DATE: ....

SCHEDULE	
5:00 AM	
6:00 AM	
7:00 AM	
8:00 AM	
9:00 AM	
10:00 AM	
11:00 AM	
12:00 PM	
1:00 PM	
2:00 PM	
3:00 PM	
4:00 PM	
5:00 PM	
6:00 PM	
7:00 PM	
8:00 PM	
9:00 PM	
10:00 PM	
11:00 PM	
12:00 PM	

MEALS

BREAKFAST:

LUNCH:

DINNER:

ACTIVITIES

NOTES

MEMORIES

ITINERARY

DATE: ....

SCHEDULE	
5:00AM	
6:00AM	
7:00AM	
8:00AM	
9:00AM	
10:00AM	
11:00AM	
12:00PM	
1:00PM	
2:00PM	
3:00PM	
4:00PM	
5:00PM	
6:00PM	
7:00PM	
8:00PM	
9:00PM	
10:00PM	
11:00PM	
12:00PM	

MEALS

BREAKFAST:

LUNCH:

DINNER:

ACTIVITIES

NOTES

MEMORIES

DATE: ....

 ITINERARY DATE: ....

SCHEDULE	
5:00AM	
6:00AM	
7:00AM	
8:00AM	
9:00AM	
10:00AM	
11:00AM	
12:00PM	
1:00PM	
2:00PM	
3:00PM	
4:00PM	
5:00PM	
6:00PM	
7:00PM	
8:00PM	
9:00PM	
10:00PM	
11:00PM	
12:00PM	

MEALS

BREAKFAST:

LUNCH:

DINNER:

ACTIVITIES

NOTES

MEMORIES

DATE: ....

 ITINERARY   DATE: ....

SCHEDULE	
5:00 AM	
6:00 AM	
7:00 AM	
8:00 AM	
9:00 AM	
10:00 AM	
11:00 AM	
12:00 PM	
1:00 PM	
2:00 PM	
3:00 PM	
4:00 PM	
5:00 PM	
6:00 PM	
7:00 PM	
8:00 PM	
9:00 PM	
10:00 PM	
11:00 PM	
12:00 PM	

MEALS

BREAKFAST:

LUNCH:

DINNER:

ACTIVITIES

NOTES

MEMORIES

DATE: ....

ITINERARY

DATE: ....

SCHEDULE	
5:00AM	
6:00AM	
7:00AM	
8:00AM	
9:00AM	
10:00AM	
11:00AM	
12:00PM	
1:00PM	
2:00PM	
3:00PM	
4:00PM	
5:00PM	
6:00PM	
7:00PM	
8:00PM	
9:00PM	
10:00PM	
11:00PM	
12:00PM	

MEALS

BREAKFAST:

LUNCH:

DINNER:

ACTIVITIES

NOTES

MEMORIES

DATE: ....

TRAVEL NOTES

TRAVEL NOTES

TRAVEL NOTES

TRAVEL NOTES

TRAVEL NOTES

⚑ TRAVEL NOTES

TRAVEL NOTES

⚑ TRAVEL NOTES

TRAVEL NOTES

TRAVEL NOTES

TRAVEL NOTES

TRAVEL NOTES

TRAVEL NOTES

TRAVEL NOTES

 TRAVEL NOTES

TRAVEL NOTES

TRAVEL NOTES

TRAVEL NOTES

TRAVEL NOTES

TRAVEL NOTES

# TRAVEL NOTES

Printed in Great Britain
by Amazon

41205834R00036